HISTORY
FOR
PEACE
TRACTS

How do we understand what was, grapple with
what is and prepare for what is likely to be,
as a nation, as a people, as a community,
as individuals?

This series is an attempt to address this question
by putting into print thoughts, ideas and
concerns of some of South Asia's most
seminal thinkers.

*In memory of Kozo Yamamura (1934–2017)*

FORTHCOMING IN 2023

IRFAN HABIB
*Nationalism in India*

KRISHNA KUMAR
*Learning to Live with the Past*

JANAKI NAIR
*Is a Single Teachable Indian Past Possible Today?*

YOUSUF SAEED
*Partitioning Bazaar Art*

DEEPA SREENIVAS
*Remaking the Citizen for New Times*

# Reimagining
# Indian Secularism

RAJEEV BHARGAVA

LONDON NEW YORK CALCUTTA

The text in this volume is an updated edition of a
lecture delivered at the 2019 History for Peace
conference 'The Idea of the Indian Constitution'.

**Seagull Books, 2023**

© Rajeev Bhargava, 2023

First published in volume form
by Seagull Books, 2023

ISBN 978 1 80309 289 8

**British Library Cataloguing-in-Publication Data**

A catalogue record for this book
is available from the British Library

Typeset by Seagull Books, Calcutta, India

Printed and bound by WordsWorth India,
New Delhi, India

# CONTENTS

*Preface*

This essay is part-scholarly, part-speculative. A reasonably complete scholarly monograph would take all relevant material into account. At least it would not leave out the most important secondary material. I am not sure I have done this. I am uncertain whether I have deployed all textual and non-textual evidence to support my conclusions. This is less true of my sections on secularism than the ones on religion. The scholarly material on it is expectedly massive and I believe that my work on religion has just begun. But having started this intellectual adventure, I thought that this was the right moment to make it public. It is politically urgent to begin a public discussion on the alien character of the category of religion in India. My goal would be accomplished not if others agree with me but if they too join me in this intellectual quest. Our thoughts on these issues must evolve together, in conversation and with reasonable disagreements.

# INTRODUCTION

For much of its history, the idea of religion was either absent or had an unstable, uncomfortable existence in India. Those who berate secularism for being alien to India must first recognize the foreignness of religion itself.[1]

This may sound very counterintuitive to many. Has not India been the land that gave birth to some of world's greatest, most ancient religions—Hinduism, Buddhism, Jainism? Is not the 4,000-year-old Rigveda a religious text? How can anyone assert that religion is a foreign idea here? But this is precisely my claim. The fact that the Rigveda was composed in the Indian subcontinent does not imply that we had religion in India. Buddha's teachings, Jain asceticism and the Upanishadic quest were unquestionably present in India's past but none of this entails the presence of religion. The category of religion provides an interpretative grid within which to place these facts, and I fear its unexamined usage misleads us into thinking of our past and present world in a way that damages our ethos and distorts our experience. For much of its past, India had religio-philosophical experiences and practices but not a larger, more comprehensive category called religion within which to subsume them. Religion came to India at a specific time in history and changed the way we came to conceptualize and experience a large chunk of our world. Until quite recently, it was an alien notion and to some extent still remains so. The concomitant idea of secular and secularism must be viewed in the same way. In what follows, I show that the distinctiveness of Indian secularism is in large part a result of our struggle with and adaptation to the Western construction of religion.

I also show that while our encounter with Western ideas of religion and secularism had forced us to reimagine secularism, in the present day even that reimagined secularism has run into problems. Can we continue to put the blame then on those critics of secularism who mistook Indian secularism for one or the other Western variants or should those of us who advocated it finally admit that the defect lies within the Indian variant itself, in its Indian-ness? I argue that the fault lies in a bit of both. Indian secularism remains badly misunderstood by both its critics and supporters but significantly, even the best supporters have failed to properly identify the full conceptual implications of the ideal. Indeed, they have not been able to rearticulate its original appeal or recapture its moral and spiritual power. Unless this is done, it will remain unattractive to those it serves best. Reimagining secularism is a task ahead, not behind us, as something already done and dusted. In a sense then Indian secularism needs to be continuously reimagined.

## INDIA'S NON-RELIGIONS

I begin by taking the reader several
millennia back to a world and time
where what we now call religion and
culture were not distinct from each
other.[2] Indeed, one might even say that
there was no religion but only cults and
cultures. Nor was there a clear division
between the divine and the natural. The
idea of gods and goddesses was around,
but they were not objects of belief or
faith. They were simply taken for
granted. Their presence in the world was
self-evident. People were oriented wholly
towards the world, to be at home in it,
rather than turned away from it. Take,
for example, India of the early Vedic

period. The Rigvedic hymns centred around sacrificial rituals (yajnas) were performed for 'wealth, rain, cattle, superiority within clan or tribe, good health, living for the proverbial 100 years, and then finding one's way to heaven'—all constituents of a this-worldly conception of human flourishing.[3] The sacrifice involved a transactional, reciprocal relationship between two classes of elites, the Rajanyas and rich householders and the Brahmins (who alone had the knowhow and thereby the authority to perform the yajna). Within the early Vedic worldview, there was no duplication of the world— there was no world other than this one. Nor was there a conception of an afterlife. Each human being was born once and died once. There was no cycle of birth and death, no reincarnation.

To attain all these this-worldly goods, ritual sacrifice needed to be performed and gods propitiated so that they intervene in this world to facilitate self-realization, conceived entirely in this-worldly terms. These cults and gods evolved over thousands of years and were viewed as eternal. In virtually all cultures of early antiquity, each god performed a function based on his or her cosmic competence. Thus, there were gods of love, war, knowledge, craftsmanship. Likewise, each god embodied an entity of potentially cosmic significance. Hence, gods of fire, rain, earth, time, sun, moon, sea or primal gods who create, destroy, preserve, and so on. The god of rain in one culture could then also acquire the name of the god of rain from another culture. This way differences continued to be viewed as irreducible and yet translatable. One might even call this feature of translatability *a theology of recognition*.[4] A second strategy widely practised in the ancient world involved the bringing together of two or three gods leading to hyphenated cosmic deities such as Amun-Re in Egypt or, later, Hari-Hara in India.[5] The two gods do not merge. They retain their individuality, but each becomes a crucial aspect of the other. Thus, Hari becomes the cosmic aspect of Hara, and Hara the local cultic aspect of Hari. Each complements the other without subsumption or domination. Ardhanarishvara too exemplifies this.

Finally, a strategy even more common in all ancient cultures involved ontological subordination of one god to another.[6] Thus one god becomes the supreme deity of which all other gods are manifestations, as Rama and Krishna become avatars of Vishnu. Or we might have a pantheon of equal gods with very diverse primal functions, and others are but his manifestations or relatives.

Each of these strategies permitted free movement across different cultures and religions. Freedom of conversion is hardly the appropriate term here. Conversion implies one's permanent departure from the worship of one god to the exclusive worship of another. But this goes against the very point of these strategies of translation, hyphenation and hierarchical assimilation. For instance, if different names refer to the same god or the same god has different cultural backgrounds, then why create a fuss about leaving one and embracing another? Indeed, why not embrace both? Here, a free movement back and forth and indeed the simultaneous commitment to all can exist. This is true both when unity is explicitly claimed (inclusive monotheism) or when it is merely implied as in polytheism. I shall call this phenomenon *sanatan sanskriti*, centred around this-worldly goods, pleasure and regulatory laws (artha, kaama and dharma). Strictly speaking, the term *religion* is inappropriate here.[7] It is best to think of it as *non-religion*.

This sanatan sanskriti, with close affinity to what Jan Assmann calls *primary religion*, and which continues to survive in India, is to be distinguished from other forms of faith and worship that emerged from disaffection with early Vedic culture, in the face of problems emanating from both natural and social causes—being at the mercy of wild natural forces, confronting disease, death, separation, violence and social oppression. Humans developed a yearning to move beyond, to transcend this world of gods and goddesses and the many troubling situations from which they are unable to deliver them. With a newly developed capacity for transcendence, they learnt to step back and look beyond life as they found it, to holistically examine their world and their own existence within it, to dispassionately see its limitations and aspire to overcome them. To bridge the gap between what they currently were and what, at their best, they could be, they strove for a vision, both personal and collective, in terms of which they could chart a journey of self-development and self-fulfilment. If the prospect of death consumed them, they sought an answer to the question 'how can we be saved in the face of death?' in salvation.

One important condition of identifying this vision was to be guided, most likely by a teacher with the requisite brilliance, insight and wisdom, one who was capable of deep influence in shaping one's character, practice and perspective on life and the world. People then began to follow the teachings, usually though not always, of a single, great teacher: a guru. They became followers of a path towards self-realization—of a *way* (marga)—and soon all those who followed the same path imagined by their common teacher develop a loose sense of community, important for self-cultivation, a practice that demands mutual learning, influence and reinforcement. Since they are primarily an ethic of self-realization, I treat margas too as non-religion.[8]

Margas grew out of sanatan sanskriti and were critical of them—as Upanishadic teachings were of the early Vedic worldview—but they do not oppose them tooth and nail. The teachings of Buddha also began by negating the sanatan sanskriti or primary religion of the Vedas, but eventually, in the lives of ordinary people, it made peace with them.[9]

## THE FIRST STEP TOWARDS RELIGIONIZATION

A speculative account of some further historical developments may be noted. A section of most communities of both sanatan sanskriti and marga took upon itself the responsibility to first systematize teachings and then give internal coherence to them. In short, they turned these teachings into intellectual doctrines (for example, the Mimansa-mediated Vedic worldview or the Advaita Vedanta of Adi Shankaracharya). Some of these, once a loose community, also acquired a doctrine-oriented, bureaucratized structure of power and status. The search for self-fulfilment now became conditional on one's belonging to this institutionalized community. Marga-based or sanatan communities now became demarcated from each other. And their members developed a reasonably sharp sense of their own distinctive identity. With these robust identities, they began to make a sharper distinction between the self and the other, began guarding the internal norms of their own ethical community more zealously, and even saw each other as competitors for, say, political patronage. I propose that this process occurred not only in India but in virtually every human society. Some degree of rigidity is found in every stable ethical community, although this is true more of its elites than its ordinary members.

## THE SECOND STEP TOWARDS RELIGIONIZATION

However, some societies, especially around Palestine, undertook other radically different moves. These societies introduced what Assmann has called an *emphatic conception of truth* into their ethical doctrine.[10] More specifically, they introduced the idea of one true God and correspondingly, the notion that all other gods are false. Not that they denied the existence of other gods, but precisely because they recognized their existence, they understood that people might be tempted to worship them. Thus, they expressly forbade the worship of these *false* gods. Recall the strategies of sanatan sanskriti or primary religions that help the translation of gods of one culture into another. In contrast, this new conceptual understanding blocked translation. Translation becomes impossible if you show the irreducible non-equivalence of the terms sought to be translated, if two terms simply cannot refer to the same entity, if only one god is true and all others false.[11] If the worlds centred on the two irreducible entities are incompatibly different, then one can either live in one or in the other, not in both. From now on, belief in one true God was accompanied by the idea that those who believe in false gods are radical outsiders—completely outside the true system of meanings, wholly excluded from the semantic universe around the one true God. This is exclusive monotheism. Although Assmann speaks of it as a secondary religion to distinguish it from primary religion, he observes that only this phenomenon really deserves to be called *religion*.

With this, a new idea of otherness was created: one who is not just a competitor but an enemy. An adherence to a true God now came with an enemy to be fought, denounced as idolaters, superstitious or as pagans. It is true of course that a fight to the finish was not the only option. The other could be brought into one's semantic universe, saved from false gods by conversion. Proselytization then became incumbent on the believer. But if persistent attempts to convert were unsuccessful then humiliating marginalization, expulsion from the community or, worse, extermination were the only other options. In short, the other was someone one could not live with: he was an existential threat. In a sense then, inter-communal or inter-religious domination became an integral part of religion. A deep conflict with other communities with radically different religious beliefs and practices became part of the definition of religion.

Equally important was to ensure that one always remained true to the doctrine and did not deviate even an inch from the true path. Any deviation was to succumb to false gods, to the devil, and therefore those who did indeed stray, i.e. differed from the orthodoxy, were also treated as enemies. Indeed, as internal enemies, they were to be treated even more harshly than radical outsiders, external enemies. To ensure that people remained continuously on the true path and maintained their belief in the true God, a crucial requirement was to have strong gatekeepers, who guarded the boundaries of the true ethical community.

This new radical otherness also brought in a new form of hatred, a new kind of violence and forms of radical exclusion that were unknown to sanatan sanskriti or to the more self-reflective guru-based communities of the marga traditions, such as the Buddhist or even very early Christian. From now on, believers were ready to break each other's heads over differences of doctrine or practice. And to smash the heads of even co-religionists who differed from doctrines as understood or defined by them.

These developments brought into existence the idea of a religion that opposed itself to everything before it. It spoke about a radical rupture, a break from the past. These are what I call *strong* secondary religions, to slightly modify Assmann's idea.[12] They are secondary because they grow out of primary religions and are strong rather than weak because they define themselves in permanent opposition to primary religions and to each other. In their self-understanding, proponents of strong secondary religions thought of their relationship with primary religion as one of antagonistic acculturation.[13] One key feature of this antagonism was that they believed that they had completely emancipated themselves from the conditions of their birth. They had transcended all political and ethical boundaries. The contours of their teachings were no longer inscribed in the institutional, linguistic and cultural conditions of the society in which they were born. This made it possible to understand themselves, to view their identity solely in terms of their doctrinal religion.

## THE THIRD STEP TOWARDS RELIGIONIZATION

These secondary religions developed another feature. In order to understand this change, a distinction must be introduced between what I have above called the ethics of self-fulfilment and the social norms of everyday conduct. By 'ethics of self-fulfilment', I mean a framework for meaningful living and dying—a full life in *this* world; swarga, jannat or heaven in another world; being forever compliant with the commands of a transcendent God; or emancipation from recurrent births and deaths (moksha or nirvana). I have referred above to these as ethically oriented margas. By 'social norms of everyday conduct', I mean rituals and ceremonies of social interaction, but even more importantly norms governing interpersonal relations—with whom one should or should not interact, whom one should or should not marry, with whom one should or should not dine, who is to perform which job in society and what the comparative significance is of these jobs. The ethics of self-fulfilment and the norms of social conduct may be so tightly connected that they form one single system. Or the connection between them may be so loose that they are seen to constitute two separate entities.

In sanatan sanskriti, the connection between an ethics of self-fulfilment and norms of social interaction was extremely loose. This meant that you could move from one ethic to another or simultaneously partake in two or more ethics without altering one's participation in social norms. For example, one could be a Jain at one time and a Buddhist at another, or be a follower of both Vishnu and Shiva, but still remain a Brahmin or a Vaishya. Ethical pluralism could go hand in hand with a stable social structure. Furthermore, violations of norms of social interaction had very little to do with the truth and falsity of religion, which was an altogether different matter, if it existed at all.

But in some strong secondary religions, such as Latin Christianity, at some stage in their development, the connection between the ethics of self-fulfilment and the norms of social interaction became very tight, so tight that one could now view them as one system.[14] No one could have a particular view of self-fulfilment and not participate in a specific set of rituals which is associated with that ethic, or not be governed by highly specific and codified norms of social interaction. To embrace an ethic was to belong to this entire system of ethics and social norms. Such comprehensiveness was unknown to non-religions. Furthermore, violation of social norms was said to result from holding false doctrines. The perfection in believing true doctrines was closely accompanied by a strict adherence to norms. Those who deviated marginally from true doctrines or deviated from social norms were inferior Christians. This was at the root of church-related intra-community or intra-religious domination. In a sense, a propensity for intra-religious domination lay at the heart of the very idea of religion. If this is how religion began to be conceived, then any society with a pluralist ethic of self-fulfilment or with a loose connection between ethics and social norms did not have a religion.

## THE FOURTH STEP TOWARDS RELIGIONIZATION

In Europe, religion acquired yet another feature. This development occurred with the breakup of Latin Christendom. Wars of religions erupted everywhere in Europe. One treaty that went some way towards stopping these wars was signed in Augsburg in 1555. The famous phrase *cuius regio, eius religio* (whose realm, his religion) summarized the central clauses of this treaty. This meant that the ruler of a territory had the right to impose his faith (Catholic or Lutheran) on his subjects, free from outside interference.[15] Thus, rulers began first to publicly release a document, the confession of faith, each propounding a rival truth, and then to enforce religious uniformity on their subjects. If subjects dissented, they only had the right to emigrate. The only other alternative was death, particularly as dissent and sedition began to coincide. Political fragmentation offered a ready solution to religious conflict: differences of faith 'were suppressed within territories, validated between them, and thus made to follow existing political lines.'[16] In this process, we see not only the birth of confessional religions but also confessional states, states that defined themselves—the ruler and his subjects—in terms of this new religious (confessional) identity. Confessional religions are state religions, brook no dissent and are committed to a version of truth as propounded by their state church. Confessionalization turned religions into political ideologies and tied them strongly to specific territories, creating proto-national states in which territorial belonging was strongly tied to specific confessional religions. Over time, religious truth was enforced by states, virtually as a state doctrine. Faiths became intolerant, teaching too doctrinaire, intellectual claims dogmatic. Religious diversity, therefore, was never an issue there—that problem had been resolved, unethically, by expulsion or execution. There was one dominant church, and the state was very closely aligned with it.

## RELIGION

To repeat, by the sixteenth and seventeenth centuries, Europe had collective entities (institutionalized communities) that were:

— mutually exclusive and necessarily conflicting;
— comprehensive;
— sought exclusive allegiance not only to their version of the truth
— but also to the state with which they had strong alliance.

This is what the term *religion* had come to refer to by this time in Europe. It had no space for non-religions because the very idea of non-religion had disappeared from European discourse. Besides, as ideas oriented towards liberty and equality grew, the term acquired a negative connotation because piety itself demanded intolerance or intra- and inter-religious domination. In a sense then, modern Western religion *is* communal. The central institution of religion, namely the church, was also seen negatively because of its socially oppressive and politically meddlesome features. In short, religion began to invite a strong protest against itself.

For this reason, a religion-centric social revolution in Europe meant:

a. breaking the monopoly of Christianity, presenting options other than dominant Christian ideas of self-fulfilment—a pluralization of ethics;

b. loosening the connection between ethics and social norms, freeing social norms from Christian ethics, building norms of social equality that transcended religious identities—secularization;

c. fighting a church that blocked secularization and pluralization, opposing the church and its *total religion* meant fighting intra-communal or intra-religious domination, a struggle for greater individualization—more meaningful individual freedoms and toleration of dissent;

d. the separation of the state from a politically meddlesome church.

Secularization and secularism, the rubrics under which these movements, projects and ideas were subsumed were a response to problems of the Western religion and its modern form. All European and North Atlantic countries in their own distinctive ways went through this phase and therefore some degree of secularization. In most, this process slowed down or was halted, and some form of compromise was reached. Given the nature of Western religions—their exclusive monotheism, the comprehensive power of their churches and their confessionalization, some degree of anti-religiosity which was equivalent to being anti-religion (features a–d) was bound to be a feature of their secularism and with good reason.[17]

## BACK TO NON-RELIGION

In India, until recently, things were different. To take one example, the connection between ethics and social norms remained very loose in Indian traditions. Because social norms and power hardly ever dictated the choice of ethics, there was greater innovation, and for this reason, ethical frameworks proliferated. People could move freely from one framework to another and sometimes participate in several without any discomfort. And yet, precisely because social norms existed independently of ethics, this very ethical flexibility went hand in hand with great rigidity within social norms. This is so because hierarchical and fixed caste relations lay at the core of these norms. Ironically, they even complemented each other; as long as one remained within the caste system, one could choose any ethical framework, any path to self-fulfilment. A person could find fulfilment in a loving relationship with Krishna, in achieving swarga, or in liberation from the cycle of rebirth and at the same time follow common norms governing unequal social relations. A person may quit a this-worldly Vedic ethic in order to lead an ascetic Jain life but all the while continue to belong to the Vaishya caste, and therefore remain enmeshed in hierarchical caste relations. This was true even for those who became Christians or Muslims; they chose a modified Abrahamic ethic but remained entrenched in the caste system.

For much of its history, India was free of exclusive monotheism or at the very least of its dominance; there were no churches to bring together doctrinal truth and dominant social norms under one wing; there was no confessionalization. Indian religions or rather *non-religions* had their share of problems, but the complete alignment of dogma, social norms and political power was not one of them. In India, non-religions did not have the comprehensiveness until perhaps the nineteenth century, when they began to turn into strong secondary religions themselves, and the idea of confessional religion did not grip the imagination of the elites until the early-twentieth century. To be sure, a few stray strands did threaten to take religious experience and practice in that direction. The Manavadharmasastra (Manusmriti) comes very close to conceiving religion in this Western sense. But contrary features in the social imaginary pulled them back, contained or steered them towards an altogether different track. Thus, the history of the subcontinent is littered with millions of individuals and groups participating in sanatan sanskriti and following one or the other margas; even developing doctrines and hierarchical structures. But the idea of a bounded community seeking exclusive allegiance was at best marginal, not centre stage. Fuzzy communities, multiple allegiances, and fluid, hybrid and composite identities were the norm. The sudden induction of the idea of full-blown confessional religions had a dramatic, somewhat disastrous impact on religious formations in India.

This is hardly surprising, given that the term *religion* was invented within

Latin Christianity to refer to a single comprehensive system. It was not easily applicable in the subcontinent where ethics and social norms do not cohere into one single whole. Yet, such is the force and sway of the term *religion* that it has been used simultaneously to refer to two relatively distinct and independent entities: ethics and a system of social norms. This has generated many problems and much confusion. Consider the following simple example from the natural sciences to grasp the absurdity of this profound misnaming. The term *water* refers to a single entity composed of two distinct elements, oxygen and hydrogen. Where the two gases are bonded together to form a single compound, the term *water* is appropriate, but we rightly use two distinct terms *hydrogen* and *oxygen* for each when the two remain separate from each other.

How utterly erroneous to call them *water* when they exist separately! Calling distinct systems of ethics and social norms in India by the common term *religion* is equally absurd. But then once a term grips the popular imagination, it is difficult to dislodge.

I might try to convince those who remain sceptical of my move to confine religion to Europe and North America by making another argument. Many scholars accept that capitalism is a modern idea. They do not deny that money, trade, market, money lending, interest, manufacturing and profit existed before capitalism. But if many of these elements existed in the past, why do they deny that capitalism did not? They do so because they claim, and rightly so, that all these elements had not come together to form a system with an explicit purpose. That is exactly my point. I do not suggest that rituals, cults, worship, prayer or hymns, gods, goddesses, myths and morally sanctioned norms did not exist in the past, but my argument is that they did not all come together to form a total system with a single dominant purpose. This 'coming together', the formation of religion as a comprehensive system is a result of a historical process that is not uniform but one that varied from place to place and time to time. It assumed a different pace in different societies. To add to this complexity, in some places, the process is far from completion. In others, it may have only just started.

# DEPLOYING 'RELIGION' IN INDIA

Another way of getting out of this hole is by using *religion* in two different senses: ethical religion and social religion, to which one might also add political religion. If we accept this, we might say that in India, a profound pluralism of ethical religions exists.[18] Yet, followers of different ethical religions participate in much the same caste-ridden social religion. More recently, political religion has also taken a robust form.

Another strategy is to use religion, in not two but four senses:

1. sanatan sanskriti
2. marga

3. religion proper (comprehensive, strong secondary religion with a propensity for intra- and inter-religious domination)
4. confessional or politicized religion

In the West, arguably, 1. and 2. virtually vanished as independent entities and were subsumed by 3. and 4. Secularism then became a struggle against every Western society's own religion.

I ask the reader to pause once again. The different uses to which I have put the term *religion* often leaves me confused, so I can well imagine how the reader would be even more befuddled. Let me attempt then to clear the mess as well as I am presently able to. Western secularism's hostile response to religion is motivated by a certain conception of it— a total exclusivist system within which a particular ethic and a specific set of social norms are tightly knit, a system which is monistic and therefore does not allow for pluralism, and that craves for state power. Some scholars with some justification say that this is a secularist construction of the term *religion* in which piety or what I have called the ethic of self-fulfilment is entirely eclipsed. But the secularist point is that the European socio-cultural milieu had made it impossible to have an independent ethical religion, to remain a non-religion or be a religion in senses 1. and 2. without simultaneously partaking in senses 3. and 4. To belong to religion in senses 3. and 4. was a condition of having the experience of religion in senses 1. and 2. For those outside religion, features 3. and 4. were all that could be seen *as* religion. This was the conception of religion in most European societies against which secularism emerged. Indeed, this is what explains the power of secularism, its motivation, original appeal and attraction.

The introduction of the category of religion in India brought the threat of subsumption of senses 1. and 2. by senses 3. and 4. Since at least the early nineteenth century, it generated contemporary Indian religions with problems similar to Western religion. These new formations tried to eclipse non-religions and when they did not succeed, coexisted with them. Contemporary Indian religions then have a certain elasticity. Not only can India, at any given point of time, have religion in each of the four senses but each religion can move quite rapidly from sense 1. to sense 4., shifting from one end of the continuum to the other. It follows that Indian secularism too has to work with this quality of contemporary Indian religions—their multiple forms and dynamism. It had no reason to have any comprehensive animosity towards contemporary Indian religions. It did not have to work against senses 1. and 2. (sanatan sanskriti and margas respectively), be against non-religions (indeed, it is entirely compatible with them), or, if we do not wish to discard the term *religion*, against the pluralism of ethical religions (Hindu, Jain, Buddhist, Islamic or Christian). But it had to resist religionization, the process by which:

— the idea of a loose community of faiths nourished by the rituals or teachings of one or more traditions is transformed not only into bounded well-demarcated communities enforcing a single set of communal norms on their members, particularly because there is a mutual-relatedness between perceived false beliefs and violation of social norms;

— comfortably cohabiting, relatively flexible groups are turned into rigid communities locked into a permanent battle with each other, i.e. rivalrous communities, to one of which all members of a society exclusively belong and which becomes the source of a rigid categorical identity.

It also had to combat politicized religion. If the term *religion* contains within itself not only intra- but also inter-religious domination, then Indian secularism unlike Western secularism becomes doubly anti-religion. This must be particularly true when sanatan sanskriti and margas (senses 1. and 2., non-religions) were converted by their spokespersons and leaders into strong secondary and eventually political religions (senses 3. and 4.). When they conformed to Western ideas of religion, Indian non-religions too became communal, i.e. began to view the interests of their community as necessarily opposed to others! This is what pained Gandhi who believed that senses 3. and 4. were perversions of religion and not religion itself. Indeed, since contemporary Indian religions are a mix of senses 1. – 4., they too had aspects of both intra- and inter-religious domination.

## PROSPECTS OF
## INTER-RELIGIOUS DOMINATION

In modern India, the idea of inter-religious domination had immediate resonance on the ground. Readers might recall that from the late 1920s, sections of Hindu and Muslim elites were sucked into what can be called a majority-minority syndrome, a diseased network of neurotic relations, so completely poisoned and accompanied by a such a vertiginous assortment of negative emotions (envy, malice, jealousy, spite and hatred) that collective delirium and cold-blooded acts of revenge, sending groups on a downward path of deeper and still deeper estrangement, were mindlessly, alternately and cyclically generated. In this condition, animosity between groups circulates freely, adding layer upon layer of grievances, and antagonistic games are played with no end in mind except the defeat and humiliation of the other. Ambedkar provides several examples:

> the 'preparations' which the Muslims and Hindus are making against each other without abatement [. . .] are like a race in armaments between two hostile nations. If the Hindus have the Benares University, the Musalmans must have the Aligarh University. If the Hindus start Shudhi movement, the Muslims must launch the Tablig movement. If the Hindus start Sangathan, the Muslims must

meet it by Tanjim. If the Hindus have the RSS, the Muslims must reply by organizing the Khaksars.[19]

A section of Muslims, it appears, had entered a state of paranoia that was only partly grounded in fears of inter-religious domination (domination by members of one religion over members of *another* religious community) but which got exacerbated and became a very real prospect for those who stayed behind in India after the formation of Pakistan.

## PROSPECTS OF
## INTRA-RELIGIOUS DOMINATION

But the majority-minority syndrome had
another consequence. In the nineteenth
century, a number of reform movements
oriented towards liberty and equality had
been initiated within Hindu and Muslim
communities. But the syndrome set off by
inter-communal rivalry forestalled these
reforms, intensifying anti-reformist
tendencies. Once again, Ambedkar grasped
this point well:

> So long as the Hindus and the
> Muslims regard each other as a
> menace, their attention will be
> engrossed in preparations for
> meeting the menace. The exigencies

of a common front by Musalmans against Hindus and by Hindus against Musalmans generate—and is bound to generate—a conspiracy of silence over social evils. Neither the Muslims nor the Hindus will attend to them even though the evils may be running sores and requiring immediate attention, for the simple reason that they regard every measure of social reform as bound to create dissension and division and thereby weaken the ranks when they ought to be closed to meet the menace of the other community.[20]

In other words, prospects of intra-religious domination (domination by members of one religious community over members of their *own* community) had also grown by the time of India's independence.

It was in such a context replete with continuing inter- and intra-religious domination that independent India had to decide the character of the newly instituted state and its relationship with religion. It had two options: either to have a polity that consolidates both forms of inter-religious domination—a patriarchal, upper-caste-dominated Hindu-majoritarian state—or to have a secular state that blocks these tendencies and tries to reduce both these forms of domination. Credit must go to the people in the Constituent Assembly for taking the second option, despite the very strong presence and availability and backing of the first. In doing so, two distinctive conceptions of political secularism were developed: *Gandhian political secularism* and *Indian constitutional secularism*.

## SECULARISM PREFIGURED: GANDHI'S COMMUNAL HARMONY

Gandhian political secularism must be understood within the context of the strong anti-religionization stance taken by Gandhi, who never wholly accepted the idea of religion rooted in the Abrahamic tradition. Yet he continued to use the term as many others did before and after him. He begins by accepting that 'there is endless variety in all religions', that there are 'interminable religious differences'. 'Some go on a pilgrimage and bathe in the sacred river, others go to Mecca; some worship him in temples, others in mosques, some just bow their heads in reverence; some read the Vedas, others the Quran.' There is, for Gandhi, not only diversity *of* religions but also diversity *within* them. '[W]hilst I believe myself to be a Hindu, I know that I do not worship God in the same manner as any one or all of them.'[21] Given this deep religious diversity, 'the need of the moment is not one religion, but mutual respect and tolerance of the devotees of the different religions.'[22] Gandhi dismissed the idea that there could ever be one religion in the world, a uniform religious code, as it were, for all human kind. Yet, 'the soul of religion is one, but it is encased in a multitude of forms [. . .] Wise men will ignore the outward crust and see the same soul living under a variety of crusts.'[23]

Unlike conceptions which presuppose the idea that oneness with significant others as well as God is achieved by abolishing or belittling the radical other, i.e. by eliminating plurality, in Gandhi's vision oneness is attained by accepting all radical others as equally significant because they variously manifest one supreme being or concept. We may not be able to do or be what others are, we may even dislike some of their beliefs and practices, but we recognize that they are translations of our own selves or of gods within each of us.[24] Thus, the moral-practical attitude of equal regard for all religions is a (practical) entailment of a deeper epistemic grasp of the fundamental unity of all religions. He says, 'whilst I hold by my own, I should hold others as dear as Hinduism, from which it logically follows that we should hold all as dear as our nearest kith and kin and that we should make no distinction between them.'[25]

This Gandhian view did not stem from strategic considerations, but was grounded in deep conviction. It is sometimes said that Gandhi's views were influenced by Jain teachings. 'All religions [a]re true and also that all ha[ve] some error in them,' he said, implying that all religions are inevitably partial, incomplete, fragmentary, so that different traditions need to complement and enrich one another rather than behave as mutually exclusive rivals. Without denying this philosophical lineage, I claim that Gandhi's views were shaped even more by the 'wisdom traditions' of the ancient world, in which gods and goddesses of each cultural region are different, yet part of the same semantic universe and therefore mutually related and translatable.[26] As a result, no culture denied the reality of the gods of another culture but always found ways to accommodate them. For instance, the god of another culture could become a member of the family, say, someone's son (Ganesha, the son of Shiva and Parvati). A new god could be created by merging half of one god with half of another (Hari-Hara). Most of all, a relation of equivalence or identity could be established between them (Shiva and Rudra), making it possible to claim that the gods of different cultures were the same, only called by different names. Gandhi was inspired by popular religious traditions, by the cultural milieu of non-religions, particularly by the habit of establishing equivalence, and he extended this insight to the all contemporary world religions. He illustrates this by a striking verse from the Guru Granth Sahib in which Guru Nanak says that God may be called by the name of Allah, Rahim and so on. Thus, 'Rama, Rahim,

Krishna, Karim are all names of the one God. *Sat Shri Akal* (God is True) is an equally potent cry.'[27]

If different names refer to the same god or the same god has different cultural backgrounds, then why create so much fuss about leaving one and embracing another? Indeed, why not embrace both, even all? If all religions are the same, movements of conversion or purification are pointless. 'The real Shuddhi movement should consist in each one trying to arrive at perfection in his or her own faith. In such a plan, character would be the only test. What is the use of crossing from one compartment to another, if it does not mean a moral rise?' Two more things follow. First, '[t]o revile one another's religion, to make reckless statements, to utter untruth, to break the heads of innocent men, to desecrate temples or mosques, *is* a denial of God.' Second, '[i]t is wrong for anyone to say that his God is superior to that of another's. God is one and the same for all.'[28]

For Gandhi, contemporary religions are conflictual but they need not generate permanent hatred or deep disharmony. Yet, when such discord occurs, Gandhi felt that a large part of the responsibility for maintaining communal harmony lies with members of the communities themselves. Communal harmony is a people-dependent notion, one that Gandhi believed was already part of popular Indian consciousness. Its realizability depends on faith in popular wisdom traditions which in turn are sustained by a certain idea of popular moral agency. When good, god-loving, ordinary men and women free from the

trappings of power, wealth and fame—
precisely what makes them ordinary and
good—get together, they release non-
violent creative energies that can improve
our world. But such energies are
jeopardized in our times by communal
politics. In such times when harmony is
disturbed and even breaks down, the
state may have to step in.

## GANDHIAN POLITICAL SECULARISM

The first Indian version that took
inspiration from Gandhi's social project
of communal harmony was believed to
be wholly homegrown and was variously
called 'sarva dharma sama bhava'. Soon
after Independence, this idea found
articulation in public discourse as
secularism, strictly speaking, *political*
secularism. The state must show 'sarva
dharma sama bhava', i.e. it must be
equally well disposed to all paths, god or
gods, all religions, even all philosophical
conceptions of the ultimate good. As an
entity separate from all religions, the
state was to ensure trust between
religious communities, to restore basic

confidence if and when it was undermined. This might happen under conditions when there is a threat of inter-religious domination.

Secularism then refers to a comportment of the state, whereby it maintains a distance from all religious and philosophical conceptions in order to promote a spirit of fraternity or a quality of sociability among religious communities, perhaps even inter-religious equality. This makes Gandhian secularism distinctive. Unlike modern Western secularisms that separate church and state for the sake of individual freedom and equality and have place for neither community nor fraternity, the Gandhian conception demands that the state be secular for better relations between members of all religious communities, especially in times when they are estranged. By speaking explicitly about fraternity between religious groups, Gandhi redefined the ends for which separation is sought. Gandhian secularism opposes inter-religious domination by proposing that all religions must be treated as equals by the state.

While the originality of this political project cannot be denied, it has often been touted as the official state-led Indian secularism, competing with and virtually eclipsing constitutional secularism. I claim instead that the Gandhian conception is largely subsumed within Indian constitutional secularism (ICS). Largely but not wholly—some features of the Gandhian ideal should have been made even more explicit in ICS. While the emphasis given to communal harmony is important, and in certain contexts sorely needed, constitutional secularism of the Indian variety has a more balanced approach to religious communities. In what follows I explain this second conception, and having traced the trajectories of both, briefly indicate where the current discourse of secularism stands and why it needs to be freshly reimagined.

# INDIAN CONSTITUTIONAL SECULARISM

ICS translates Gandhian political secularism, an adversary of inter-religious domination, into the language of rights. It does so by ensuring that religious communities that are smaller in number have rights that protect them from potential disadvantages. At the same time, it also goes beyond inter-religious issues to incorporate a transformative agenda aimed at reducing intra-religious domination. Its opposition to all forms of institutionalized religious domination makes ICS distinctive.

What then is the relationship between a constitutional state and religion that it wishes to partially transform? What is the relationship of our Constitution to contemporary Indian religions? Unlike Europe, where people have to fight for the pluralization of ethics, here:

— We strive to conserve the immense pluralism of our ethical religions, to act against any attempt at religious homogenization or exclusion. The Indian Constitution performs this *conservative* function. This pluralism cannot survive inter-religious domination.

— By preventing a tight connection between social norms and ethical religion, the Indian Constitution, wherever possible, discourages the formation of *religion* as conceived in exclusionary monotheistic traditions, something as totalizing as Latin Christianity had been or Saudi Islam now is. It does not permit modern, confessional religion.

— Finally, its main objective is to destroy what is at the core of India's dominant social religion—its deeply hierarchical caste system and its gender-based hierarchies.

Allow me to elaborate. Indian constitutional secularism is distinctive because without being anti-religious or religion in senses 1. and 2. (sanatan sanskriti and margas; see pp. 40–41), it fights institutionalized religious domination in both forms: inter-religious and intra-religious. This conception was a genuine innovation. I would like the reader to grasp its conceptual inventiveness by furnishing several examples that show that it can work as a model.

Consider the following:

— A tax is imposed on Hindus but not on Muslims.

— Churches are attacked by intolerant Hindus or Muslims.

— Catholic schools are subsidized by the state but Hindu, Muslim, Protestant and Jewish schools are not.

— A person called Hussain is unable to get a house on rent.

All these involve discrimination, exclusion, marginalization, oppression or humiliation on grounds of religion, but victims and perpetrators come from different religious communities. We call this *inter-religious* domination.

Take another set:

— A woman is burnt at the stake because she is believed to be a witch.

— A man is stoned to death for heresy.

— A woman is not allowed to enter a temple because she is more than 15 and less than 55 years old, a time span in which she is menstruating and hence 'polluted'.

— A man from the lowest caste, believed to be an untouchable, is not allowed to take water from the well.

In all these cases, some person is discriminated against, excluded, marginalized, intimidated, oppressed or humiliated on grounds of religion, or somewhere along the chain of reasoning behind this persecution, a religious rationale is cited. Moreover, in each of these cases, both the victim and the perpetrator are from the same religious community. We call this *intra-religious* domination. Intra-religious domination takes other forms too: when Ahemdias are deemed to be non-Muslims and their places of worship prevented from being called *mosques*; when Catholics are persecuted by Lutherans; or when a Shaivite temple is desecrated by Vaishnavites.

The point I wish to make through these examples is that secularism must be seen as a critical social perspective not against religiosity, religio-philosophical experiences or even against loosely organized religio-ethical communities (against non-religions), but against all forms of institutionalized religious domination described above (or against religion as constructed in sixteenth- and seventeenth-century Europe, though it was long in the making). Political secularism is a narrower part of this larger social perspective which claims that our states should be designed in order to reduce both these forms of domination. This requires that the state is not captured by a particular group or is not aligned to a particular religious community. Some form of separation between the two must exist.

Now this understanding of secularism as explicitly against *two* forms of institutionalized domination is an Indian invention. A number of features mark Indian secularism:

— A distinction is drawn between the identity of the state which is made largely independent of all religions and an important but limited sphere where religious freedom is guaranteed and religion officially recognized (Articles 25–30).

— The qualification for citizenship qua membership in the state is made wholly independent of religious affiliation but a small number of important rights are mediated by membership in religious communities (Articles 26–30).

— The state is required to be equally (well- or ill-)disposed to all religions. No religion is supposed to be politically dominant or favoured by the state.

— More interestingly, contemporary religion (a mix of senses 1.–4.; see pp. 40–41) is understood to be a complex, morally ambiguous phenomenon—some aspects of which deserve respect and non-intervention, other aspects that deserve respect requiring positive intervention from the state, and still others active disrespect and state-intervention (ban on untouchability, potential to reform personal laws, etc.).

In short, there is no blanket disrespect towards contemporary religions nor an unqualified respect for them, but rather an attitude of critical respect. This is crucial, given the virtual impossibility of distinguishing the religious from the social, as B. R. Ambedkar famously observed, something that he must have perceived in the transformation of Hindu margas into comprehensive religions. Every aspect of religious doctrine or practice cannot be respected. Respect for religion must be accompanied by critique.

This attitude of critical respect finds expression in law and public policy in the form of what I have called *principled distance*. In India, the metaphor of separation, then, was unpacked differently: not taken to mean strict exclusion of religion from state but viewing the boundaries between state and religion as drawn less rigidly, more flexibly. The state keeps a distance from all religions. It engages with or disengages from them, engages with them positively (by helping them) or negatively (inhibiting them), precisely in order to treat them as equals. It even treats them differently depending upon which of these in a specific context promotes complex values of equality, liberty, fraternity (alternately which of them reduces inter- or intra-religious domination). It is this subtle, complex, less formulaic and more judgement-dependent character that makes Indian secularism conceptually and theoretically distinctive, different from other models extant elsewhere. Allow me to substantiate this claim.

Broadly speaking, what might be called the idealized French model interprets separation to mean one-sided exclusion. In this idealized form, it is anti-religious because it doesn't officially recognize religious communities, tries to remove religion from the public domain, privatizes it and very often shows active disrespect for religion. In a sense, it attempts the most comprehensive denunciation of modern religion, making no distinction between senses 1., 2., 3., and 4. But Indian secularism doesn't do this. It continues to see the kernel in the external shell of modern religion. It does not push religion outside the public domain. The Constitution recognizes religious communities particularly in the section on minority rights. And when the Constitution talks about giving funds to all religious communities non-preferentially, it also obviously recognizes (though not explicitly) the majority Hindu community.

The other model is the idealized American model. There, instead of one-sided exclusion, there is mutual exclusion—state and religion have their own respective areas of jurisdiction; the state cannot interfere in religion and religion cannot interfere in the state. In a sense, American secularism protects modern religion (senses 1. and 2. subsumed by 3. and 4.) from state intervention. That, of course, is something we can't have in India. If we did, then we would not be able to ban untouchability, nor would we be able to have legislation allowing the entry of Dalits into temples or the access to wells. Besides, any kind of intervention in religion-based personal laws would be impossible.

The third model, termed *modest secularism* by Tariq Modood, is followed by the rest of Western Europe.[29] There, after the initial hostility to church or religion, what we now have are relatively religion-friendly states. This comes as a shock to many who think of Europe as a haven of secular humanism, which in some sense it is because it does defend individual rights, conceived independently of one's religion. Thus, there is no possibility of the non-religious to discriminate against the religious on any grounds. These aspects of European states are praiseworthy. Nonetheless, what we do not remember is that many of these states continue to have institutional links with one church. Though these states are in some aspects secular, they continue to favour not just their own religion but one church of that religion. Now, this European arrangement should not really surprise us because secularism arose in societies which had already been religiously homogenized. Religious diversity, therefore, was never an issue there—that problem had been unethically resolved. There was one church, and the state was very closely aligned with that church. Such states have gone furthest to prevent intra-religious domination but simply do not explicitly acknowledge that they are communal, i.e. remaining hidden within them is an unadmitted aspect of persisting inter-religious domination.

To sum up, in much of the West, over time, changes began to take place in the social, economic and political arena and people began to find the church to be socially oppressive and politically meddlesome. They had *unchurching* struggles to separate the church from the state. At issue here was intra-religious domination—inter-religious domination was not an issue because religious diversity was not. And this is true even today because it was not until the twentieth century that religious diversity returned to Europe, thanks to immigration from former colonies and globalization. And European Christian faiths were thrown together with pre-Christian and post-Christian faiths, leading to both religious diversity and its accompanying tensions.

We can see more clearly now how the Indian ideal is very different from European models. And all those critics who have talked about Indian secularism being Christian and Western have only got hold of a tiny bit of its story. Those who were faced with all the problems left behind by colonization had to reimagine secularism. They found the doctrinal, ideological and theoretical formulations of mainstream Western secularisms to be highly restricted and inadequate, for while they are equipped to deal with the domination of the secular by the religious or confront one aspect of religion-related domination (intra-religious), the inter-religious aspect slips easily from their sight. For instance, India's diverse religious landscape made the policy of favouring one religion (as in Europe or indeed the Middle East, including Israel) very difficult to implement. Besides, mainstream models developed in Europe and the North Atlantic allow either too much or too little intervention in the domain of religion. States with a history of ideological support for these models have deliberately breached what these models enjoin, for pragmatic or principled reasons, but have invariably failed to manage or accommodate all religions within their territory. India needed a different model of secularism to cope with all religion-related problems. Secularism then simply had to be reimagined. But a re-imagination of secularism was and continues to be virtually impossible if we remain in the grip of these 'Western' formulations and practices. Paradoxically, a version of secularism that is widely believed to be radically anti-religion, namely Western secularism, is only partially so, and the other viewed as accommodative of religion, the Indian version, is wholly and doubly anti-religion.

I have said that Indian secularism has to be reimagined but since secularism in India has already been reimagined during our anti-colonial struggle that led eventually to the birth of the Indian

Constitution, to reimagine it today means a partial retrieval of the original formulation. The idea of religion, a comprehensive system that includes both inter- and intra-religious domination, must be resisted. In addition, reimagining secularism today demands that we confront the problems that plague the current discourse of Indian secularism.

# THE CURRENT DISCOURSE OF INDIAN SECULARISM AND ITS PROBLEMS

I accept that forces have been unleashed more recently that attack the secular ethos of our society in a manner that is more blatant and persistent, but it would be foolish not to admit that, wittingly or unwittingly, deliberately or unintentionally, various social and political groups have been chipping away at the secular edifice, so that gradually its moral power and legitimacy have been eroded. Indeed, my focus is on the discourse of secularism led by secularists themselves. The moral and spiritual power of secularism, its attraction and appeal, vanish when those who defend it lose their way. Though I attend to the conceptual and narrative-related flaws in the understanding and defence of secularism, I do not for a moment suggest that they contributed more to the crisis of secularism than external factors. Far from that. But such internal factors account more for the loss of its moral appeal and power which is my focus in this essay.

Where did we go wrong with the discourse of secularism? As part of this answer, I briefly state five propositions. My first point relates to something important that is almost completely absent from our discourse of secularism—the religionization of ethics and faiths—a process that was fast-tracked and consolidated in Europe during and after the wars of religion in the sixteenth and seventeenth centuries, but which did not properly emerge in India at least until the nineteenth century.[30] The history of the subcontinent is littered with millions of individuals and groups having taken steps to form multiple ethical religions, sometimes with fluid and at other times with more rigid and exclusive attachments, but a full-blooded idea of a bounded community of a tightly knit system of ethics and social norms, seeking exclusive allegiance, was at best marginal, not centre stage. Fuzzy communities, multiple allegiances and fluid, hybrid and composite identities were possibly the norm. This also means that inter-religious domination was not an integral part of religio-philosophical experiences and practices. As mentioned above, the introduction of the idea of fully grown comprehensive religion—the Western idea of religion—had a dramatic, somewhat disastrous impact on early religious formations (non-religions) that still persist in India.

Yet, this process of religionization is still reversible. Older religious formations are still very much around and in some places even have a fairly stable presence. It follows that religionization is still incomplete and therefore still unstable. Reversing this religionization of ethics and traditions (and ritual and philosophy) should be one of the primary tasks of the secular project in India. Secular practice has partially recognized this, in its invocation of Kabir, for example, or a figure such as Lal Ded in Kashmir and more recently, Sai Baba of Shirdi, but the issue has never found a forceful, general and normative formulation. I believe these religious currents must be actively supported by society and state.

However, since one must acknowledge at least a partial religionization of religious experiences and philosophical outlooks, constitutional secularism both tries to prevent the formation of contemporary Indian religions and oppose them where they have taken root.

With this I move to my second claim: those who defend secularism have frequently lost sight of the whole point behind a secular state, what secularism stands for. Most Indian secularists have frequently defended not the complex, sophisticated Indian constitutional model that simultaneously opposes both forms of institutionalized religious domination, but instead some very limited and partial version of it or, worse, one or the other Western variants. They have alternatingly defended a secularism that is anti–sanatan sanskriti and anti-margas—alienating the ethically religious by failing to treat them as citizens worthy of equal respect, sometimes putting their force behind an a-religious secularism—failing to understand that no modern state can keep itself aloof from religion in any of the four senses, especially in places like India where religion cannot easily be separated from the social and the cultural. They have also sometimes chosen to support a vulgar form of Gandhian multi-religion-respecting secularism that has a high propensity to tolerate indefensible socio-religious practices and that cries foul every time the state intervenes in religion. This has got defenders of secularism into a mess. They have allowed the state to intervene in religion when they should not have, to intervene when restraint was desperately needed and frequently continued to respect aspects of religion not worthy of respect and disrespect those facets that deserved respect. An acute understanding of the complex and variegated ways in which inter- and intra-religious domination persists in the interstices of Indian society has been elusive and therefore has been challenged, if at all, only half-heartedly.

A related point has to do with the precise value of the word *secular* in relation to liberal democracy. It is sometimes argued that the term, first used in the Kesavananda Bharati case in 1973 and introduced explicitly into the Preamble of the Constitution only in 1976, is redundant. While secularism is against discrimination or exclusion only on the basis of religion, liberal democracy is against all forms of discrimination. The term *liberal democracy* subsumes secularism and is therefore sufficient. Some Indian scholars argue for the sufficiency of Articles 14–16 and 19 of the Constitution that guarantee individual liberty and equality, making it liberal-democratic. This may have been adequate in societies that are religiously homogeneous, but not so in societies with deep religious diversity. To substantiate my argument let me introduce a counterfactual.

What if Europeans had to institute a liberty-loving, equality-caring state as soon as religious wars erupted in the sixteenth century, in order precisely to end them and not centuries later when in fact they did? What if there was not much of a time lag between religious wars and the growth of a serious commitment to the values of liberty, equality and fraternity? Had this been so, demands for ending the religious persecution of dissenters and preventing religious homogenization would have been immediate. How else could a state live up to ideals of liberty and equality? Moreover, the dynamics of a multi-religious society is such that religion would not have lost salience, as it did in the late-nineteenth century. Then, instead of getting rid of religious dissenters and minorities, a general consensus might have been sought to prevent their domination by the majority religious community. Had multiple religious identities been part of the European social climate, a commitment to equality would have compelled European states to give impartial public *recognition* to all religions. Such states would be secular precisely in the sense that Indians conceived it—something with which to fight not just religious fanaticism and intra-religious oppression but also the domination of one religion by another. They would have been forced to call themselves not just *liberal* (subsuming within it secular in the European sense) but also *secular* in the sense defended by Gandhi, Nehru and Ambedkar where it designates impartial public recognition to all religions. It is because religion-sensitive recognition is necessary in limited domains in countries such as India that secularists should hold their nerve and fight for the word *secular*.

My third proposition: that Indian secularism is not anti-religious (not against religion in the sense of sanatan sanskriti or marga, i.e. ethical religions) is widely understood. But not that it is simultaneously against both forms of institutionalized religious *domination*. How did this misunderstanding grow? First, these two struggles—the one against inter-religious domination (a defence of minority rights, opposition to majority and minority communalism) became separated from the other, intra-religious domination (religion-related patriarchy and caste domination; fanaticism, bigotry and extremism). Then, this intra-religious dimension was ejected from the meaning of secularism and, much to the detriment of its overall value, secularism began to be identified, by proponents and opponents alike, exclusively with the defence of minority rights, as a device for the protection of minorities, especially Muslims. This opened the door for viewing secularism first as a tool to protect the interests of Muslims and Christians, of no relevance to Hindus, and then for twisting it to appear as pro-Muslim and anti-Hindu. The strength of Indian secularism—its advocacy of minority cultural rights—was easily made to appear as its weakness and the burden of its defence, rather than be shared by all citizens, fell on the minorities and 'pro-minority' secularists. This is unfair, partly because it puts the entire burden of defending secularism on minorities and on secularists who are sensitive to the rights of minorities. Secularism is needed as much to protect Hindus, Muslims and others from intra-religious domination— from their fanatics, orthodoxies and extremists, and from proponents of religion-based caste and gender hierarchies. Indeed, there are good reasons to believe that a causal nexus exists between a failure to address intra-religious domination, in particular caste hierarchies, and the intensification of inter-religious domination. The more one ducks the problem of caste hierarchies by taking refuge in a discourse of upper-caste-led Hindu unity, the more the scapegoating of Muslims and Christians and the deeper the abyss into which secularism falls.

My fourth proposition is to do with secularism's frequent failure to distinguish communitarianism from communalism. Communitarianism simply notes that an individual is at least partly defined by his or her religious and philosophical commitments, community and traditions. Therefore, it is entirely appropriate to claim that one is a Hindu, Muslim, Sikh, Christian, atheist and so on, to take legitimate pride in one's community or be ashamed of it when there is good reason to. Communalism is different. Here one's identity and the existence and interests of one's community are viewed and even defined as necessarily opposed to others. It is communal to believe or act in a way that presupposes that one can't be a Hindu without being anti-Muslim or vice-versa. Communalism is communitarianism gone sour. It is to see each other as enemies locked in a permanent war with one another. Every decent Indian national should be against communalism. But no one should decry legitimate forms of communitarianism. It is simply wrong to conflate communitarianism with communalism, or the communitarian orientation of non-religions, of sanatan sanskriti and margas, with the communal orientation of religions, including contemporary Indian religions.

The conflation of communitarian and communal in India has often meant that secular persons with a Hindu background or identity have not found a way of articulating the religious or socio-religious interests of Hindus without sounding communal and have often appeared to have defended Muslim faith and interests mala fide, as if in doing so, their being communal was permissible given the vulnerability of minorities in a representative democracy dominated by Hindus. The fact is that there is nothing wrong in articulating and defending some Hindu, Muslim and Christian interests when they do not come into conflict with one another.

Attention must also be drawn to another problem of Indian secularism. Our education system often fails to distinguish religious instruction and religious education. No publicly funded school or college should have religious instruction, best done at home or in privately funded schools; but reasonable, decent education should include elementary knowledge of all religious traditions. A deeper understanding of these traditions is vital, for it would make young students aware of their strengths and weaknesses, and discern what in them is worth preserving or discarding. But Indians come out of their education system without a deeper, critical understanding of their religio-philosophical traditions. As a result, a defence of our own religious traditions or a critique of others' is shallow, lacks weight and is frequently mischievous.

My final point is perhaps the most important. In the last 40 years or so, ever since Indira Gandhi played the 'Hindu card' in the early 1980s, we have developed a secularism that is a travesty of the original idea—what I call 'party-political secularism', an odd, nefarious 'doctrine' practised by political parties, particularly the so-called 'secular forces'.

This secularism has dispelled principles from the core idea and replaced them with opportunism; opportunistic distance from all religious communities is its slogan. It has removed *critical* from critical respect and reduced the idea of respect to making deals with the loudest, most fanatical, orthodox and aggressive sections of every religious group. Thus, political parties keep off religion or intervene as and when it best suits their party or electoral interests. This has led to the unexpected and cynical unlocking in 1986 of the Babri Masjid/Ram Janmabhoomi temple, the orthodoxy-appeasing curtailing of women's rights in the law overturning the Shah Bano judgement in 1986 and the indefensible banning of *The Satanic Verses* in 1988— all by the Congress Party—and to electoral deals with the likes of Ahmed Bukhari by all and sundry. It has even made states complicit in communal violence. This is also a fertile ground for majoritarian Hinduism whose spokespersons can question all the deal making and opportunism of 'secularists' without examining their own equally unethical practices. The word *all* is replaced by *majority*: respect only the majority religion; never criticize it, but recklessly demonize others. Here, the state is rid of the corrupt practice of opportunistic distance not by restoring principled distance but magically abolishing distance altogether. This is untrammelled majoritarianism masquerading as secularism, one that opposes 'pseudo-secularism', as the BJP put it.

Alas, electoral politics has sidelined or corrupted our constitutional secularism and the rise of Hindutva has made the Gandhian part of constitutional secularism redundant. To be fair, electoral politics breeds opportunism. If one's only aim is to win, to do so by any means is always tempting. But it is here that we need the courts, a free press, an alert citizenry and civil society activists to move in, to show a mirror to these parties and tell them what they can and cannot do. At present, Indian constitutional secularism is swallowed up by this party-political secularism, with not a little help from the opposition, media and the judiciary. Moreover, since it came to power in 2014, the BJP's majoritarian 'secularism' has done much to undermine the democratic and institutional conditions of real secularism. With the abrogation of the Kashmir-related Article 370, the introduction of the severely discriminatory Citizenship Amendment

Act that adds a religious test to the procedure of granting citizenship, the bewildering court judgement on the Ayodhya dispute and the brazenly partisan handling of the 2020 Delhi communal riots following the Shaheen Bagh protests, constitutional secularism has been forced to go on the ventilator.

Indeed, secularism has already been pronounced dead by many. I suggest that this judgement is premature and unsound because it does not take a long-term view. In my view, two crucial moves are needed to kickstart the discourse and practice of secularism. First, a shift of focus from a politically led project to a socially driven movement for justice. Second, a shift of emphasis from inter-religious to intra-religious issues. Recall the birth of the majority-minority syndrome in the 1920s. Today, a century later, after the formation of Pakistan and the rise of majoritarianism, Indian Muslims appear to have opted out of this syndrome. When this happens, the syndrome implodes. The result is neither open conflict nor harmony, simply an exiled existence for Muslims in their own homeland.

Remember the other debilitating consequence of this syndrome: all dissent within the community is muzzled and much needed internal reforms are stalled. If so, the collapse of the syndrome unintentionally throws up an opportunity. As the focus shifts from the other to oneself, it may allow deeper introspection within, multiple dissenting voices to resurface, create conditions to root out intra-religious injustices and make its members free and equal. After all, the Indian project of secularism has been thwarted as much by party politics as by religious orthodoxy and dogma.

For the moment, the state-driven political project of secularism and its legal constitutional form appear to have taken a hit. But precisely this 'setback' can be turned into an opportunity to revitalize the social project of secularism. Since the Indian state has failed to support victims of oppressions sanctioned by religion, a peaceful and democratic secularism from below provides a vantage point from which to carry out a much-needed internal critique and reform of our own respective religions, to enable their compatibility with constitutional values of equality, liberty and justice. A collective push from young men and women untainted by the politics and ideological straightjacketing of the recent past may help strengthen the social struggle of emancipation from intra-religious injustices. Those who most benefit from upholding these constitutional values, the oppressed minorities, Dalits, women, citizens sick to death with zealotry or crass commercialization of their faiths must together renew this project.

I am not suggesting that secularists must hereby ignore inter-religious issues. But having itself produced disharmony, it is surely beyond the capacity of the current state to restore communal harmony. But distance, freedom from mutual obsession, give communities breathing space. Each can now explore resources within to construct new ways of living together. The issue here is not a simple retrieval of older, failed modes of religious toleration. The political project of secularism arose precisely because religious toleration no longer worked. Needed today are new forms of socio-religious reciprocity, crucial for the business of everyday life and novel ways of reducing the political alienation of citizens, a democratic deficit whose ramifications go beyond the ambit of secularism.

# CONCLUSION

I am worried that the multiple distinctions I have introduced in this essay may not have dispelled the confusion in the mind of the reader. I shall therefore yield to the temptation of providing a short summary of my argument.

I began by making a distinction between non-religions (sanatan sanskriti and margas) and religions, the doctrine-saturated, sharply demarcated, mutually exclusive, comprehensive social systems, often backed by political power.

For much of its history, India had sanatan sanskriti and margas, i.e. religio-philosophical perspectives and experiences (non-religions that at best took the first step towards becoming religions). From the late eighteenth century onwards, these non-religions began to be modelled on Abrahamic, more particularly modern Western religions. This process of turning from non-religions to religions is what I have termed religionization. When religionized, religio-philosophical practice and experience become conditional upon exclusive membership in a sharply demarcated community, grounded in the belief in a true doctrine. And other communities, anchored in falsehood, are viewed as enemies to be fought (the term *communalism* is used in India for this phenomenon, though this communal aspect is integral to all contemporary Indian religions, including Hinduism).

At the same time as the process of religionization began to gain momentum in India, religion, particularly its tendency to perpetuate intra-religious domination, was strongly challenged in Europe. In the Western world, sanatan sanskriti and margas had long disappeared or had been marginalized. That left clear battle lines to be drawn between secularism and one dominant religion. The two were locked in a fierce duel over the protection of the autonomy of the state and the individual in a religiously homogeneous world. Largely absent from their public domain were not only other religions, but also the diversity of religio-philosophical experience outside mainstream religion. In India, non-religions never went into oblivion. They lived side by side with newly emergent religions. Indian secularism had no reason to be hostile to them. Indeed, it still enjoins everyone to respect all of them. This is why religious pluralism is an integral part of Indian secularism.

The emergence and continuing presence of religion (all of them in their contemporary forms) rightly invited hostility from some Indian secularists. But to have opposed sanatan sanskriti and margas (non-religions) was a mistake. To keep repeating this mistake perpetuates a profound misunderstanding of Indian secularism. To be sure, Indian secularism goes beyond Western secularism and is doubly hostile to religion. It is against not only intra- but also, more frontally, against inter-religious domination, something, as I have mentioned earlier, Western secularism does not deal with or does so inadequately. This complex, seemingly ambivalent stance towards all contemporary religions is the defining feature of Indian secularism. It accommodates and respects all non-religions and is decidedly against both forms of institutionalized religion-related dominations. To be for non-religions and against religions, to expect the state to protect non-religions and to undermine religions—that is the distinctiveness of Indian secularism. Remembering this is part of reimagining it.

## Acknowledgements

Rich and complex ideas grow in our heads with cumulative encounters. Among the many from whom I have benefitted in meetings and conversations for nearly three decades now, four deserve special mention: Charles Taylor, Jose Casanova, Nilufer Gole and Tariq Modood. Others who mustn't be omitted here are Tani Bhargava, Sudipta Kaviraj, Javed Akhtar, Neeladri Bhattacharya, Alok Rai and Vanya Bhargav. Without the general support of Aranyani and Sanjeev, and now, increasingly, the delicious camaraderie of Miran, no intellectual work is possible. My thanks to all of them.

## Notes

1   The inspiration for a thorough questioning of the category of religion comes from William Cantwell-Smith, *The Meaning and End of Religion* (New York: Macmillan Press, 1962).

2   In what follows, my ideas on religion have been shaped by my reading Jan Assmann's work mentioned below.

3   Stephanie W. Jamieson and Michael Witzel, 'Vedic Hinduism' [1992] in Arvind Sharma (ed.), *The Study of Hinduism* (Columbia, SC: University of South Carolina Press, 2003), pp. 65–113. An expanded version of the essay is available online: bit.ly/43uuXRD (last accessed: 9 June 2023).

4   Jan Assmann, *Of God and Gods: Egypt, Israel, and the Rise of Monotheism* (Madison: University of Wisconsin Press, 2008), p. 13.

5    Assmann, *Of God and Gods*, p. 58.

6    Assmann, *Of God and Gods*, pp. 58–62.

7    This must not be confused with what in Hinduism is termed *sanatan dharma*.

8    By non-religion, I mean something that is *not* religion while at the same time is not defined independently of religion. It is not necessarily *anti*-religion. For example, non-governmental organizations are organizations that *not* governmental but not necessarily *anti*-government and are not defined independently of governmental organizations. Other examples are non-profit or nonfiction. But *non* can also mean the reverse of or the negation of something, for example the term *non-violence*.

9    Early teachings of Jesus Christ might also be seen in this way—critiquing the then-extant primary religion as well as another secondary religion, the Jewish religion.

10   See Assmann, *Of God and Gods*, p. 3.

11   See Assmann, *Of God and Gods*.

12 Assmann makes a distinction between primary and secondary religions. I find it useful to make a further distinction within secondary religions between strong and weak secondary religions.

13 See Jan Assmann, *The Price of Monotheism* (Redwood, CA: Stanford University Press, 2010), p. 2.

14 This move was not taken by Early Christians until much later. In my understanding, Early Christianity was more like a marga than a comprehensive religious system.

15 Benjamin J Kaplan, *Divided by Faith: Religious Conflict and the Practice of Toleration in Early Modern Europe* (Cambridge, MA: Harvard University Press, 2007).

16 Kaplan, *Divided by Faith*.

17 Nandy appears to take little cognizance of this story. For him, secularism is a consequence of the development of modern states. As he puts it, 'Since the seventeenth century modern Western ideology of the state has required the state to be secular by

separating religion and state.' This secularism, for him, comes in one form everywhere and marks out an area of public life where religion is not admitted and confined instead to the private life of individuals. Public life must be managed by science. Religion is a threat to this rational management. See Ashis Nandy, 'The Politics of Secularism and the Recovery of Religious Tolerance' in Rajeev Bhargava (ed.), *Secularism and its Critics* (New Delhi: Oxford University Press, 1998), pp. 321–44.

18  See Rajeev Bhargava, 'Nehru against Nehruvians: On Religion and Secularism', *Economic and Political Weekly* 52(8) (2017): 34–40.

19  B. R. Ambedkar, *Writings and Speeches*, VOL. 8 (Mumbai: Education Department, Government of Maharashtra, 1990), p. 246.

20  Ambedkar, *Writings and Speeches*, VOL. 8, p. 236.

21  M. K. Gandhi, *The Way to Communal Harmony* (Ahmedabad: Navajivan Publishing House, 1963), p. 39.

22  Gandhi, *Way to Communal Harmony*, pp. 40–41.

23  Gandhi, *Way to Communal Harmony*, p. 41: 'I saw that there was a fundamental unity moving amidst the endless variety that we see in all religions, viz., truth and innocence.'

24  Gandhi, *Way to Communal Harmony*, p. 21.

25  Gandhi, *Way to Communal Harmony*, pp. 22, 57. He also says, 'My Hindu instinct tells me that all religions are more or less true. All proceed from the same God but are imperfect because they have come down to us through imperfect human instrumentality' (p. 58).

26  See Jan Assmann, 'All Gods are One: Evolutionary and Inclusive Monotheism' in *Of God and Gods*, pp. 53–75.

27  Gandhi, *Way to Communal Harmony*, p. 42.

28  Gandhi, *Way to Communal Harmony*, p. 43.

29  Tariq Mahmood, 'State-Religion Connections and Multicultural Citizenship' in Jean L. Cohen and Cécile Laborde (eds), *Religion, Secularism, and constitutional Democracy*

(New York: Columbia University Press, 2015).

30  To be sure, a few strands here and there did threaten to turn in that direction. Dharmashastric Brahmanism and currents in Islam inspired for instance by the leadership of Ahmad Sirhindi. But contrary features in the social imaginary are likely to have pulled them back, contained them or steered them on an altogether different track.